HIKING THROUGH THE FOREST

Find and circle the hidden pictures.

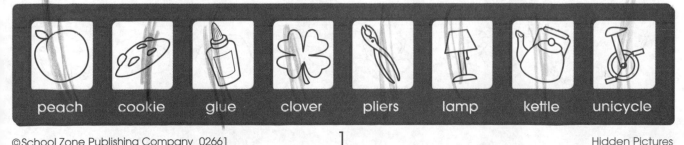

peach   cookie   glue   clover   pliers   lamp   kettle   unicycle

Find and circle the hidden pictures.

| medal | trident | scorpion | antlers | mask | walnut | cowboy hat | dove |

2

Find and circle the hidden pictures.

arrow | apple | lipstick | cloud | fork | hat | safety pin | dumb-bell

AHOY, MATES!

Find and circle the hidden pictures.

| envelope | seven | tongs | spider | lipstick | baseball bat | laddle | wrench |

pepper　　shoe　　watermelon　　guitar　　hotdog　　apple　　olive　　camera

Find and circle the hidden pictures.

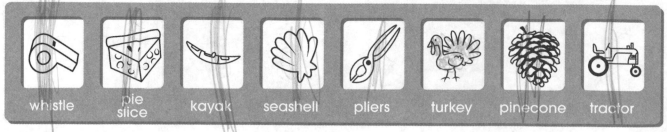

| whistle | pie slice | kayak | seashell | pliers | turkey | pinecone | tractor |

HALL OF MIRRORS

Find and circle the hidden pictures.

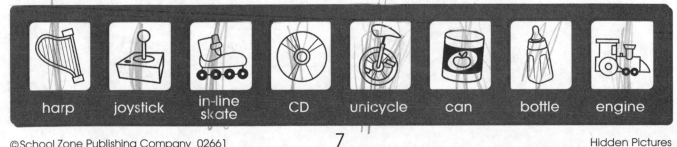

| harp | joystick | in-line skate | CD | unicycle | can | bottle | engine |

Hidden Pictures

Find and circle the hidden pictures.

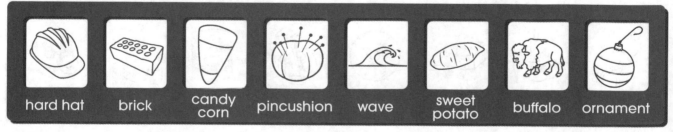

hard hat   brick   candy corn   pincushion   wave   sweet potato   buffalo   ornament

Find and circle the hidden pictures.

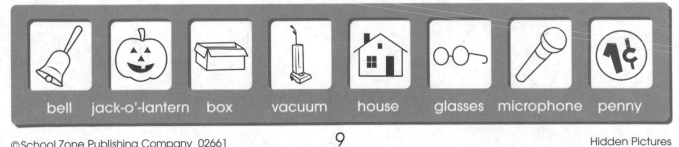

bell   jack-o'-lantern   box   vacuum   house   glasses   microphone   penny

Find and circle the hidden pictures.

| lemon | lotion | lightning bolt | dumbbell | pillow | watermelon | nail | orange |

lightbulb   taco   candy corn   magnifying glass   rocket   snake   milk carton   acorn

    Hidden Pictures

UNDERWATER ADVENTURE

Find and circle the hidden pictures.

fence   pear   scooter   pretzel   campfire   snake   palm tree   necktie

THE BIG CHEESE

Find and circle the hidden pictures.

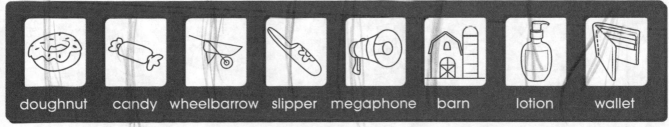

doughnut   candy   wheelbarrow   slipper   megaphone   barn   lotion   wallet

Find and circle the hidden pictures.

| hammer | lightning bolt | purse | sock | pencil | cap | baseball | journal |

A BOWL OF FUN

Find and circle the hidden pictures.

teddy bear   peanut   barrel   dress   neckace   pipe   bat   cookie

Hidden Pictures

Find and circle the hidden pictures.

bed · brick · comb · tire · stool · yo-yo · wagon wheel · map

CONSTRUCTION ZONE
KEEP OUT

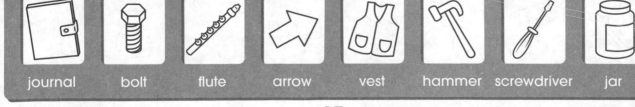

journal   bolt   flute   arrow   vest   hammer   screwdriver   jar

Hidden Pictu

Find and circle the hidden pictures.

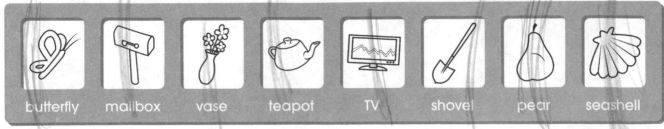

butterfly · mailbox · vase · teapot · TV · shovel · pear · seashell

Find and circle the hidden pictures.

| hamburger | fire | paintbrush | ribbon | fire extinguisher | football | snail | submarine |

19

PUPPY PARADE

Find and circle the hidden pictures.

sock   drumstick   paddle ball   envelope   helmet   yo-yo   arrow   pear

Find and circle the hidden pictures.

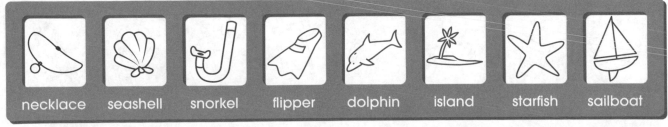

| necklace | seashell | snorkel | flipper | dolphin | island | starfish | sailboat |

21

Hidden Pictures

Find and circle the hidden pictures.

home plate | glue | watermelon | pizza slice | music player | footprint | lightbulb | puffin

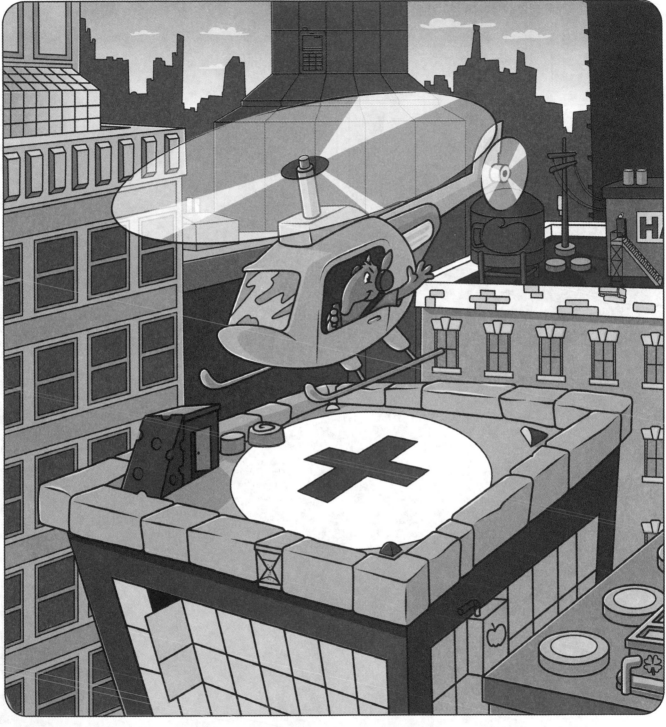

Find and circle the hidden pictures.

couch   cinnamon roll   cheese   boxing glove   juice box   hourglass   cell phone   clover

Hidden Pictures

Find and circle the hidden pictures.

lock   tire   arrow   comb   vitamin   tennis ball   satellite dish   pacifier

WELCOME HOME!

Find and circle the hidden pictures.

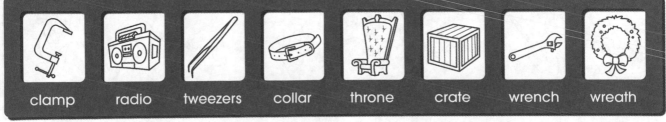

clamp radio tweezers collar throne crate wrench wreath

Hidden Pictures

WHALES ON THE GO

Find and circle the hidden pictures.

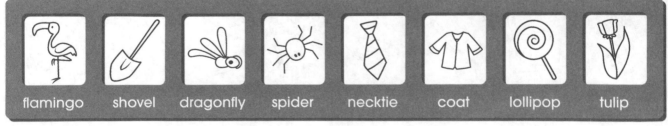

| flamingo | shovel | dragonfly | spider | necktie | coat | lollipop | tulip |

Find and circle the hidden pictures.

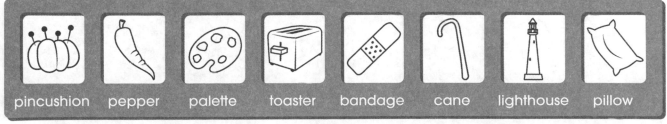

pincushion · pepper · palette · toaster · bandage · cane · lighthouse · pillow

27

Hidden Pictures

Find and circle the hidden pictures.

| fish | cork | pacifier | sweet potato | candy | spoon | iron | shoe |

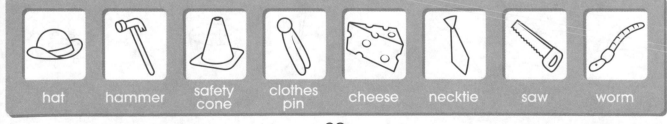

hat   hammer   safety cone   clothes pin   cheese   necktie   saw   worm

Hidden Pictures

Find and circle the hidden pictures.

| stocking cap | apple | paintbrush | cookie | broom | bowl | paper clip | spaceship |

Find and circle the hidden pictures.

| pitcher | locket | clownfish | blimp | cannon | squid | atom | hook |

Hidden Pictures

Find and circle the hidden pictures.

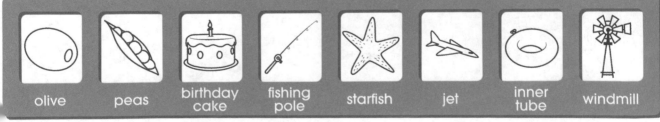

| olive | peas | birthday cake | fishing pole | starfish | jet | inner tube | windmill |

ELEPHANT EXPLORER

Find and circle the hidden pictures.

pants   saw   pail   leaf   sailboat   spatula   crown   headphones

Find and circle the hidden pictures.

| apple | chair | tulip | bee | bird | barrel | hat | boot |

necktie   palette   pie slice   horn   cowboy hat   diamond   jelly bean   mushroom

Hidden Pictu

Find and circle the hidden pictures.

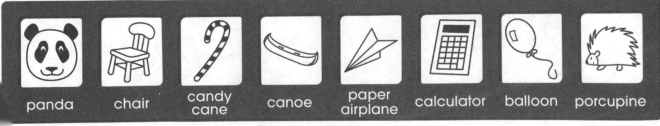

| panda | chair | candy cane | canoe | paper airplane | calculator | balloon | porcupine |

Find and circle the hidden pictures.

kite   rope   straw   bird bath   wrench   bread   pot of gold   popcorn

Hidden Picture

Find and circle the hidden pictures.

bee sandwich ornament stop sign bird tape measure drum pinwheel

Find and circle the hidden pictures.

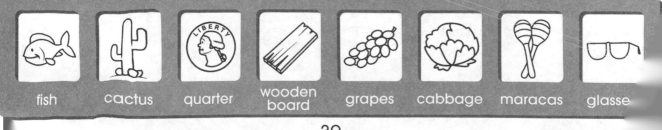

| fish | cactus | quarter | wooden board | grapes | cabbage | maracas | glasse |

AMUSEMENT PARK FUN

Find and circle the hidden pictures.

bug   grapes   book   chest   squirrel   ladder   balloon   television

Find and circle the hidden pictures.

hotdog mug horn glasses battery match horseshoe whistle

Find and circle the hidden pictures.

accordion   cork   lug wrench   hot air balloon   coal cart   bottle   horse   clock

PLAYFUL PUPPY

Find and circle the hidden pictures.

baseball bat | seal | bowling ball | apron | milk carton | moon | lamp | tennis racket

Find and circle the hidden pictures.

bread   lettuce   saw   teapot   button   eggplant   bow tie   newspaper

pretzel · toothbrush · bee · sock · bottle · mug · cloud · microphone

45

FARMYARD WAKE-UP CALL

Find and circle the hidden pictures.

| hand | alligator | rabbit | seeds | barrel | boomerang | spring | pogo stick |

Find and circle the hidden pictures.

comb   battery   pencil   gift   doughnut   glass   ring   envelope

47

BRIGHT BUDDIES

Find and circle the hidden pictures.

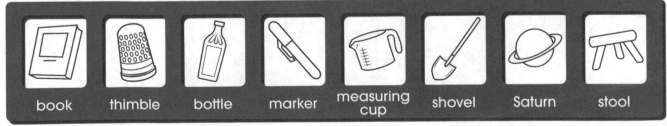

| book | thimble | bottle | marker | measuring cup | shovel | Saturn | stool |

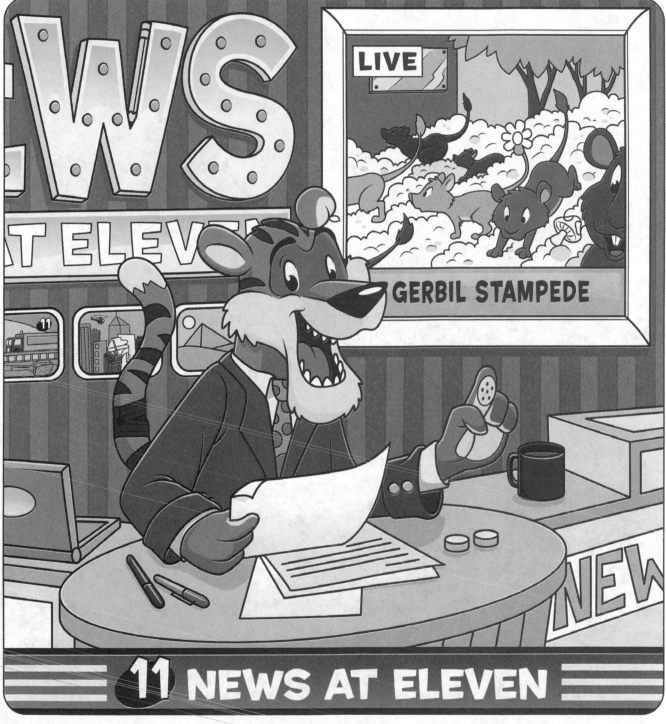

Find and circle the hidden pictures.

mushroom cracker brush shorts peach piano pencil flower

Find and circle the hidden pictures.

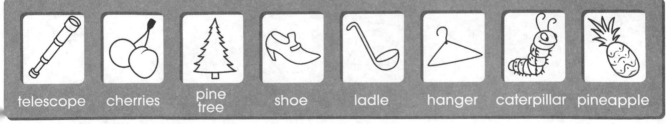

telescope   cherries   pine tree   shoe   ladle   hanger   caterpillar   pineapple

Find and circle the hidden pictures.

| briefcase | binoculars | flute | laptop | radish | tooth | pig | iron |

FOREST FRIENDS

Find and circle the hidden pictures.

oon   straw   lipstick   canoe   acorn   bowl   guitar   heart

HORSES IN THE STABLE

Find and circle the hidden pictures.

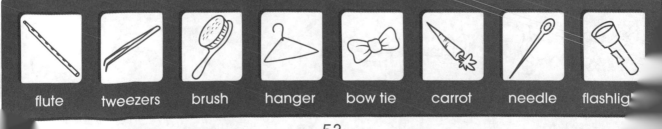

flute	tweezers	brush	hanger	bow tie	carrot	needle	flashlig

Find and circle the hidden pictures.

| rolling pin | duck | ship | pie | pan | yield sign | hat | boot |

Find and circle the hidden pictures.

| doghouse | tongs | suit | mug | cactus | abacus | soap | seven |

Hidden Pictures

Find and circle the hidden pictures.

wrench | bell | battery | cucumber | top hat | moon | purse | ghost

56

baseball cap · baseball · spoon · seeds · spider · cat · radish · rolling pin

Hidden Pictures

Find and circle the hidden pictures.

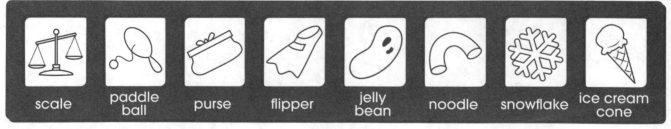

scale | paddle ball | purse | flipper | jelly bean | noodle | snowflake | ice cream cone

TURTLE TIME

Find and circle the hidden pictures.

ladybug   moon   picnic basket   chess piece   squirrel   cucumber   dollar   thermometer

Hidden Picture

Find and circle the hidden pictures.

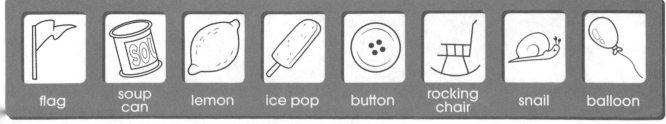

| flag | soup can | lemon | ice pop | button | rocking chair | snail | balloon |

SUNKEN SHIP SURPRISE

Find and circle the hidden pictures.

| battery | treasure chest | sock | clover | snowman | bow tie | heart | safety cone |

Find and circle the hidden pictures.

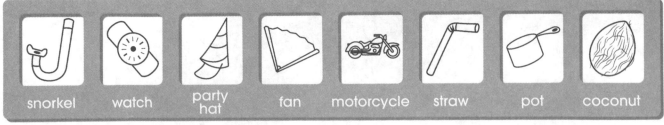

snorkel watch party hat fan motorcycle straw pot coconut

Find and circle the hidden pictures.

| screwdriver | cowboy hat | smiley face | saw | ring | CD | pyramid | bee |

Find and circle the hidden pictures.

| feather | wrench | cucumber | orange | wheelbarrow | chair | fork | arrow |

MONSTERS UNDER YOUR BED

Find and circle the hidden pictures.

butterfly   mushroom   bowling pin   milk carton   clam   salt shaker   banana   cherries

Find and circle the hidden pictures.

yo-yo   whale   popcorn   paper   semitruck   feather   table   candy

Find and circle the hidden pictures.

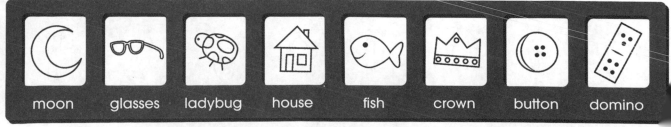

moon   glasses   ladybug   house   fish   crown   button   domino

Hidden Pictu

Find and circle the hidden pictures.

seashell · candle · magnet · bottle · push pin · earring · lamp · mailbox

Find and circle the hidden pictures.

| tuna can | magnifying glass | sailboat | pie slice | leaf | lemon | squirrel | pot |

Find and circle the hidden pictures.

| plate | crayon | hand | peanut | sun | baseball bat | rose | salt shaker |

MUD BATH

Find and circle the hidden pictures.

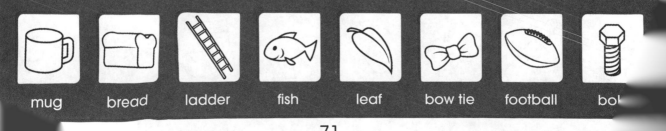

| mug | bread | ladder | fish | leaf | bow tie | football | bol |

Find and circle the hidden pictures.

| peach | marker | cane | bandage | vase | sock | plane | whale |

MOVIE:
SWAMP MONSTER 3
DATE:
JULY 3
DIRECTOR:
D. McGus
0621
SCENE:
M24

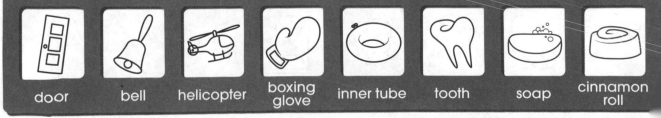

door   bell   helicopter   boxing glove   inner tube   tooth   soap   cinnamon roll

Hidden Pict

FALL FUN

Find and circle the hidden pictures.

carrot   mitten   pizza slice   strawberry   hourglass   square ruler   shovel   balloon

Find and circle the hidden pictures.

baseball cap   cucumber   pliers   book   surfboard   bandage   hockey stick   box

Find and circle the hidden pictures.

| paintbrush | bird | eggplant | taco | credit card | party hat | watch | guitar |

Find and circle the hidden pictures.

vase | fishing pole | bucket | igloo | horseshoe | hammer | chair | ice cream cone

Find and circle the hidden pictures.

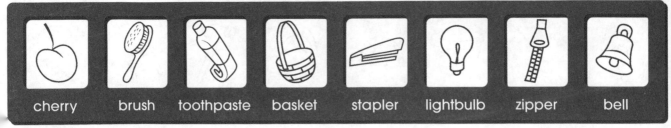

cherry   brush   toothpaste   basket   stapler   lightbulb   zipper   bell

Find and circle the hidden pictures.

| tomato | lipstick | lemon | cloud | starfish | ace | barn | CD |

Hidden Pictures

CHANNEL 6 NEWS

Find and circle the hidden pictures.

hard hat   paintbrush   vacuum   pencil   juice box   safety pin   table   hook

nail   noodle   key   wooden board   book   straw   bone   eggplant

Find and circle the hidden pictures.

butterfly   cupcake   telescope   umbrella   spoon   hot dog   basketball   shark

Find and circle the hidden pictures.

toothbrush   snail   asparagus   bow   milk carton   tennis ball   pot   snowman

MOUNTAIN CLIMBING ADVENTURE

Find and circle the hidden pictures.

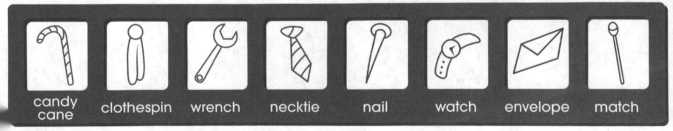

| candy cane | clothespin | wrench | necktie | nail | watch | envelope | match |

SPRING'S FIRST FLOWER

Find and circle the hidden pictures.

needle   spatula   bus   butterfly   acorn   mushroom   computer mouse   horn

Find and circle the hidden pictures.

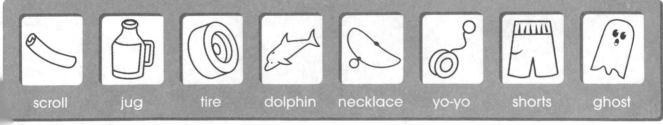

| scroll | jug | tire | dolphin | necklace | yo-yo | shorts | ghost |

Find and circle the hidden pictures.

armchair bicycle clam sweater pancakes oil can moth covered wagon

SCHOOL PLAY

Find and circle the hidden pictures.

| mailbox | ice pop | lamp | canoe | carrot | pillow | football | pear |

Find and circle the hidden pictures.

ant   couch   popcorn   plate   pot   cloud   lock   flower

WHO WOULD TRY FLY PIE?

Find and circle the hidden pictures.

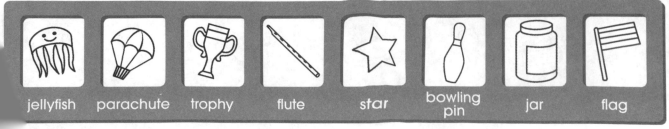

jellyfish parachute trophy flute star bowling pin jar flag

FRIENDLY FARMER

Find and circle the hidden pictures.

boomerang   hat   baseball glove   pants   watermelon   drumstick   orange   sock

Hidden Pictures

ORANGUTAN ISLAND

Find and circle the hidden pictures.

| boomerang | bottle | coconut | ribbon | ice cream cone | telescope | hammer | banana |

push pin   umbrella   juice box   paper airplane   necktie   feather   lime   seashell

93

Find and circle the hidden pictures.

| bread | megaphone | dragonfly | crown | hamburger | brush | hat | onion |

stocking cap | spatula | slice of cake | birthday cake | shirt | pizza slice | comb | key

OUTER SPACE EXPLORATION

Find and circle the hidden pictures.

| eggplant | die | flashlight | ice pop | lock | drum | celery | canoe |

96